HAL•LEONARD
INSTRUMENTAL
PLAY-ALONG

AUDIO
ACCESS
INCLUDED

PLAYBACK+
peed • Pitch • Balance • Loop

VIOLA
TOP HITS

T0066172

Audio arrangements by Peter Deneff

To access audio visit:
www.halleonard.com/mylibrary

Enter Code
4362-4188-6603-4679

ISBN 978-1-4950-6580-4

HAL•LEONARD®
CORPORATION

7777 W. BLUEMOUND RD. P.O. BOX 13819 MILWAUKEE, WI 53213

Visit Hal Leonard Online at
www.halleonard.com

ADVENTURE OF A LIFETIME

VIOLA

Words and Music by GUY BERRYMAN,
JON BUCKLAND, CHRIS MARTIN,
WILL CHAMPION, MIKKEL ERIKSEN
and TOR HERMANSEN

BUDAPEST

VIOLA

Words and Music by GEORGE BARNETT
and JOEL POTT

To Coda

D.S. al Coda
(no repeat)

CODA

mf

DIE A HAPPY MAN

VIOLA

Words and Music by THOMAS RHETT,
JOE SPARGUR and SEAN DOUGLAS

EX'S & OH'S

VIOLA

Words and Music by TANNER SCHNEIDER
and DAVE BASSETT

FIGHT SONG

VIOLA

Words and Music by RACHEL PLATTEN
and DAVE BASSETT

HELLO

VIOLA

Words and Music by ADELE ADKINS
and GREG KURSTIN

LET IT GO

VIOLA

Words and Music by JAMES BAY
and PAUL BARRY

LOVE YOURSELF

VIOLA

Words and Music by JUSTIN BIEBER,
BENJAMIN LEVIN and ED SHEERAN

ONE CALL AWAY

VIOLA

Words and Music by CHARLIE PUTH,
BREYAN ISAAC, MATT PRIME,
JUSTIN FRANKS, BLAKE ANTHONY CARTER
and MAUREEN McDONALD

PILLOWTALK

VIOLA

Words and Music by LEVI LENNOX,
ANTHONY HANNIDES, MICHAEL HANNIDES,
ZAYN MALIK and JOE GARRETT

STITCHES

Words and Music by TEDDY GEIGER,
DANNY PARKER and DANIEL KYRIAKIDES

VIOLA

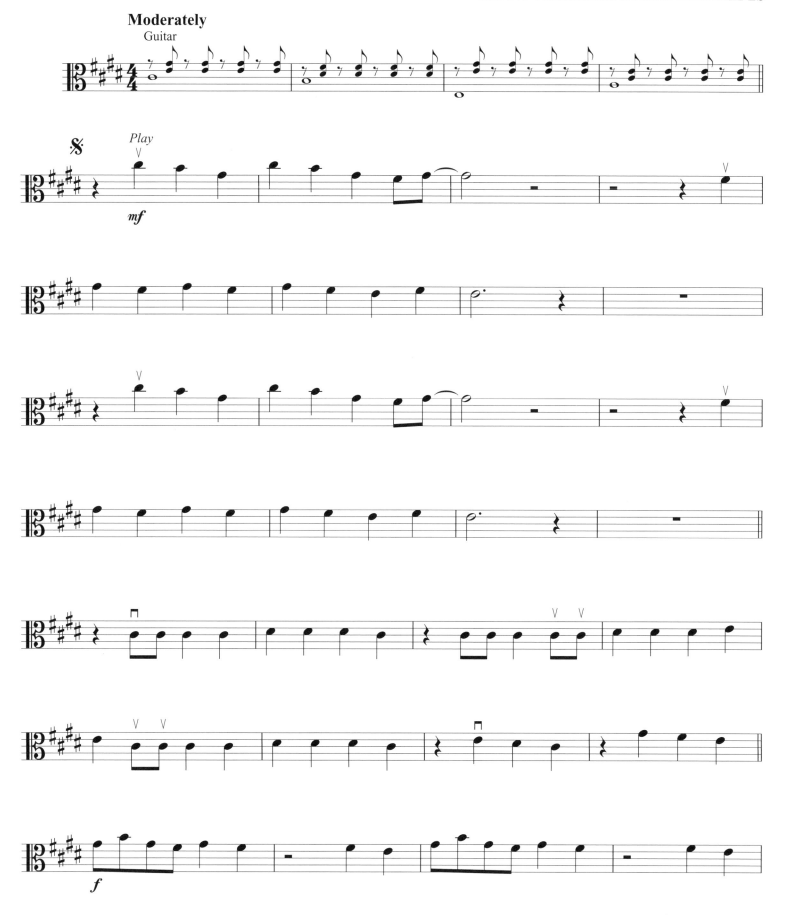

WRITING'S ON THE WALL

from the film SPECTRE

VIOLA

Words and Music by SAM SMITH
and JAMES NAPIER